Comparing People From the Past

William Caxton and Tim Berners-Lee

Nick Hunter

raintree

D0256340

Raintree is an imprint of Capstone Global Library Limited, a company incorporated in England and Wales having its registered office at 7 Pilgrim Street, London, EC4V 6LB – Registered company number: 6695582

www.raintreepublishers.co.uk
myorders@raintreepublishers.co.uk

Edited by Clare Lewis and Linda Staniford
Designed by Philippa Jenkins
Original illustrations © Capstone Global Library Ltd 2015
Picture research by Gina Kamme
Production by Victoria Fitzgerald
Originated by Capstone Global Library Ltd
Printed and bound in China

ISBN 978 1 406 28990 9 (hardback)
18 17 16 15
10 9 8 7 6 5 4 3 2 1

ISBN 978 1 406 28995 4 (paperback)
19 18 17 16 15
10 9 8 7 6 5 4 3 2 1

British Library Cataloguing in Publication Data
A full catalogue record for this book is available from the British Library.

Acknowledgements
We would like to thank the following for permission to reproduce photographs: CriaImages.com: Jay Robert Nash Collection, 12; Dreamstime: Alexander Kirch, 15, Martinmark, 24; Getty Images: Gallo Images/Danita Delimont, 8, Hulton Archive/Culture Club, 20, 26, Hulton Archive/Epics, 10, Hulton Archive/Val Wilmer, 14, Photo Researchers, cover (left), Robana/British Library, 17, Time & Life Pictures, 4, 28, Universal Images Group/UIG, 5, Science Faction/Superstock, 29; Glow Images: Superstock/Michael Grecco, 25; iStockphotos: jpa1999, 9, xenotar, 11; Newscom: Getty Images/AFP/FABRICE COFFRINI, 19, Getty Images: AFP/LEWIS WHYLD, 21, PacificCoastNews/Jean Catuffe, 27, Polaris/Rick Friedman, 6, cover (right), REUTERS/Denis Balibouse, 18; North Wind Picture Archives, 13; Science Source: Photo Researchers, Inc./SPL, 16; Shutterstock: Andre Viegas, 22, Oleg Golovnev, 23, Syda Productions, 7.

Every effort has been made to contact copyright holders of material reproduced in this book. Any omissions will be rectified in subsequent printings if notice is given to the publisher.

Contents

Some words are shown in bold, **like this.** You can find out what they mean by looking in the glossary.

Who was William Caxton?

William Caxton was born in Kent, England in 1422. In 1476 he set up a **printing press**, which printed the first books in English.

Although Caxton was an important person of his time, there are not many pictures of him.

Before printing, most books were handwritten by **monks**.

Caxton learned about printing when he lived in Europe. Printing was much quicker than writing and many more books were produced. So for the first time, ordinary people had books to read.

Who is Tim Berners-Lee?

Tim Berners-Lee is one of the most important inventors of the modern world. He was born in London in 1955. Berners-Lee works as a computer scientist.

This photo of Tim Berners-Lee was taken in 2013.

These people are using phones and tablets to access the World Wide Web.

Berners-Lee invented the World Wide Web. Using the Web, computers can share words and pictures instantly around the world. In just a few years, the Web changed the world.

Making new discoveries

As a young man, Caxton moved to London to work for a **merchant**. He later became a successful merchant himself. He travelled to many parts of Europe, including Cologne in Germany.

Merchants would visit other countries to buy and sell goods.

Johann Gutenberg created the first printed book in 1455.

The **printing press** had been invented a few years earlier by German Johann Gutenberg. In Cologne, Caxton learned how to work the new printing presses.

Berners-Lee's parents had worked on some of the earliest computers. He studied science at Oxford University. After university, he had a job writing computer software.

Berners-Lee graduated from Oxford University in 1976.

CERN is a giant laboratory where scientists from around the world work together.

Berners-Lee went to work at CERN laboratory in Switzerland. He worked with some of the world's best scientists. He realized that computers could help scientists to share ideas and **communicate**.

How were their times different?

During Caxton's lifetime, people knew almost nothing about the world outside their local area. No one in England had visited parts of the world such as the Americas and Australia.

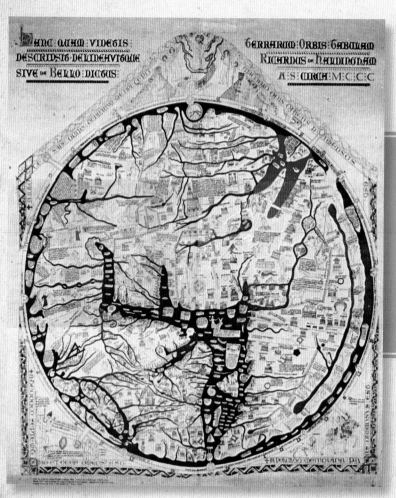

This map shows what many people thought the world looked like in Caxton's time.

Most ordinary children did not learn to read and write. They usually worked on the land from a young age. Caxton was one of the lucky ones; his parents sent him to school.

When Tim was growing up, people could talk to others around the world by phone. The first astronauts landed on the Moon when Tim was a teenager.

Phones have changed a lot during Berners-Lee's life.

How is this computer different from the ones you now use?

During the 1970s, the first **personal computers** were invented for use in homes and offices. Computers could be linked together to make networks.

What did they do?

Around 1474, Caxton set up his own **printing press** in Bruges, Belgium. He printed the first book in English. Later, he moved to Westminster, London and started a printing press there.

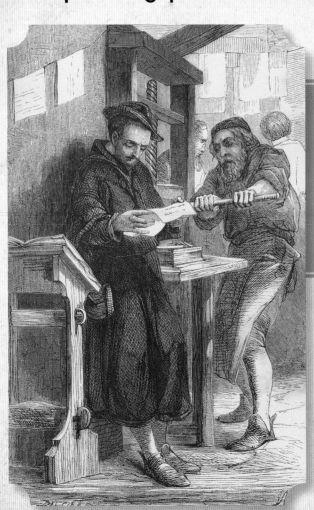

We know that Caxton rented a shop for his printing press in 1476.

One of the first books Caxton printed was Geoffrey Chaucer's *Canterbury Tales.*

Caxton printed more than 100 different books. It took a very long time to prepare the printing press for each new book. However, it was much easier than writing books out by hand.

Berners-Lee wanted to find a way for computers all over the world to **communicate** with each other. In 1989, he worked out a special computer language that would make this possible.

Berners-Lee showing the computer he used to invent the Web.

World Wide Web

http://info.cern.ch/hypertext/WWW/T

The World Wide We... ✕

The WorldWideWeb (W3) is a wide-area hypermedia information retrieval initiative aimin

Everything there is online about W3 is linked directly or indirectly to this document, inclu

Frequently Asked Questions .

What's out there?
    Pointers to the world's online information, subjects , W3 servers, etc.

Help
    on the browser you are using

Software Products
    A list of W3 project components and their current state. (e.g. Line Mode ,X11 Viola

Technical
    Details of protocols, formats, program internals etc

Bibliography
    Paper documentation on W3 and references.

People
    A list of some people involved in the project.

History
    A summary of the history of the project.

Berners-Lee's first website was very simple.

On 6 August 1991, Berners-Lee used this language to set up the first website. Other groups and developers started to create websites of their own. This was the start of the World Wide Web.

19

Who helped them?

Caxton needed money and help from powerful **nobles** to produce his books. Caxton had to make sure he pleased nobles, kings and queens. He included the names of these supporters in his books.

Caxton even knew the King of England, Edward IV.

Berners-Lee and the inventors of the internet receiving a prize for their work from Queen Elizabeth II.

Berners-Lee could not have invented the World Wide Web alone. Other inventors created the global network of computers called the **internet**. People use the internet to visit websites.

How did they change the world?

By 1500, there were **printing presses** all over Europe. Before the printing press came along, only the rich could afford books. Caxton's printing press meant that ordinary people could learn to read and write.

Printed books could be collected in libraries for anyone to read.

Printed books carried the works of scientists and thinkers to a wide audience.

Caxton's printing press allowed anyone to print their ideas. Printed books were often in English rather than **Latin,** a language used mostly by **monks.** The English language began to be used more widely.

Twenty years after Berners-Lee's first website, more than two billion people were using the World Wide Web. They could find information instantly and **communicate** with friends around the world.

The invention of the World Wide Web made the world feel much smaller.

Larry Page and Sergey Brin invented Google to help people search the Web.

The Web changed many industries. Books, films and music can now be delivered directly to all kinds of digital devices. Huge companies make lots of money by helping people use the Web.

Did they become rich and famous?

Caxton was already a rich **merchant**. He sold his books to rich **nobles** to make money. His fame came later when people realized how the **printing press** had changed the world.

This picture shows nobles visiting Caxton's printing shop to order new books.

Berners-Lee appeared at the opening ceremony of the London Olympic Games in 2012.

Berners-Lee made his invention free for anyone to use, so he did not make great riches from it. He has become famous for his invention, and was knighted by Queen Elizabeth II in 2004.

Comparing William Caxton

William Caxton

Born	1422
Died	1492
Career	Apprentice to a London **merchant**; successful merchant in Europe; printer

Greatest achievement

Printed the first book in English and set up England's first **printing press**

Fascinating fact

Caxton used his knowledge of French, **Latin** and Dutch to translate many books into English.

Famous people living at the same time

- Joan of Arc (French heroine, 1412–1431)
- Edward IV (King of England, 1442–1483)
- Christopher Columbus (explorer, 1451–1506)

WILLIAM CAXTON

1400   1500   1600   1700

and Tim Berners-Lee

Sir Tim Berners-Lee

Born 8 June 1955

Career Studied physics at Oxford University; computer scientist

Greatest achievement

Invented the World Wide Web

Fascinating fact

Tim loved trains as a child and learned about electronics by playing with a model railway.

Famous people living at the same time

- Steve Jobs (computing pioneer and businessman, 1955–2011)
- Barack Obama (US President, 1961–)
- J.K. Rowling (author of *Harry Potter* stories, 1965–)

TIM BERNERS-LEE

1800   1900   2000

Glossary

communicate share information or ideas with other people

internet huge network connecting billions of computers around the world

Latin language of the Romans, which was the language used by the English Church and government in Caxton's time

merchant someone who buys and sells goods

monk member of a religious community

noble rich and powerful person from a high social class

personal computer computer that can be operated by an individual in a home or office

printing press machine that is used to produce many copies of a book or other document

Find out more

Books

1000 Inventions and Discoveries, Roger Bridgman (Dorling Kindersley, 2006)

The Printing Press (Tales of Invention), Louise and Richard Spilsbury (Raintree, 2011)

The Science Behind Communication, Casey Rand (Raintree, 2012)

Tim Berners-Lee, Damian Harvey (Franklin Watts, 2014)

Websites

www.bl.uk/onlinegallery/onlineex/landprint/chaucer/
Find out more about Caxton and the books he printed on the British Library website.

http://info.cern.ch
The first website, created by Berners-Lee. How does it compare to your favourite website?

www.web.mit.edu/invent/iow/berners-lee.html
Discover more on this website about how Berners-Lee invented the World Wide Web.

Index